Contents

INFOTECH

E-mail

NB: an asterisk (*) in the text
denotes an entry in the
Useful lists and information
section.

1 Introduction

The purpose of this book is to clarify:

- what is meant by text manipulation (TM);
- the kind of learning that it promotes;
- its use within various classroom settings;
- techniques for setting up TM activities and embedding them in tasks.

In discussing text manipulation, I shall refer to the various exercise types as 'activities'. I shall use the word 'task' to mean a set of related activities which the student is required to complete. For example, a group of students might be asked to listen to a recording of a radio news report, make notes on the main points in the report and of the vocabulary. They might then be asked to complete a gapped text using appropriate vocabulary from their notes. The text manipulation activity is gap filling. It is situated within a broader, multi-skill task.

Throughout the book I will consider the kind of learning which TM can promote, provide ideas for its exploitation to achieve a wide range of learning outcomes, offer examples of its use and give practical advice on setting up tasks which incorporate TM.

2 Some definitions

WHAT IS TEXT MANIPULATION?

2

Text manipulation (TM) means different things to different people. It will be helpful, therefore, if we begin by a definition of what is meant by TM in this book. TM essentially encompasses a range of computer-based activities during which students make changes to a previously written text. Such activities include the following:

- sequencing words, sentences and/or paragraphs;
- replacing existing words;
- inserting additional words;
- gap filling, including cloze tests;
- unscrambling words or chunks of text;
- reconstructing a text in part or in its entirety.

In short, TM provides students with linguistic problem-solving activities which, if well set up, motivate and promote lasting language learning. Well designed activities usually include some form of information gap and/or information transfer from one medium to another. Successful use of TM relies on the extent to which it is integrated with other media and with other course activities which precede and follow it. It will enhance students' knowledge and/or use of language, depending on the design of the task within which the TM activity is located. TM activities, in particular substantial text reconstruction, can help to develop both fluency and accuracy in that they require students to produce appropriate words, in the correct form. For the purposes of this book, fluency is taken as meaning the production of words and phrases appropriate to the context within an acceptable time span, while accuracy is taken as meaning the production of the words and phrases in the correct form.

TM has been the mainstay of computer assisted language learning (CALL) for some fifteen years and numerous software packages have been produced which include one or more of the activities listed above. This proliferation is a reliable indicator of the value placed on TM by teachers and students. Despite the advent of multimedia and CD-ROMs, TM software continues to be a world-wide best seller, far outstripping its ostensibly more sophisticated rivals. There is no doubt that TM activities can be used to support a very analytical approach to language learning where knowledge of the target language is seen as of more importance than the active use of the language. However, it can be used equally successfully to support a more communicative approach where both accuracy and fluency are valued. The learning outcomes likely to be achieved derive from the design of the task within which the TM activity is situated, not from the TM activity itself.

COMPUTER-BASED AND PAPER-BASED TM

As you can see from the TM activities listed above, the majority can also be done using paper. The exception is text reconstruction which is virtually impossible to do except with a computer. TM activities set up using dedicated packages have the following advantages over paper:

3

- They usually incorporate automatic feedback to student input, either by 'marking' their answer right or wrong and/or providing them with a clue based on their input.

- Students can usually edit their input before submitting it to the computer for 'marking' and make subsequent attempts based on the feedback received.

- It is comparatively easy to set up differentiated tasks using the same text.

- In sequencing activities, there is no risk that the strips of paper will blow away!

- Activities look as fresh as the day on which you created them.

- The use of IT continues to motivate students, provided that the activity within which it is used is perceived as valuable by the student.

- If properly documented, computer-based TM activities which provide feedback and which can be done in the computer room provide a valuable resource when cover for an absent colleague is provided by a non-linguist.

INFOTECH

Text manipulation

WORD PROCESSORS AND DEDICATED PACKAGES

TM activities can be set up using a conventional word processor, or a dedicated package. Dedicated TM software usually includes an authoring component which enables teachers to provide their students with texts and related activities which are entirely in keeping with the demands of their course, their existing knowledge and skills, and their ability to use the target language. This same degree of control over content is also present when a word processor is used to set up the activities. The essential difference is that, for the most part, dedicated TM software provides students with immediate feedback or feedback on demand while, in normal circumstances, activities set up in a word processed document are unlikely to include automatic feedback, although some form of feedback can be provided in a file to be accessed by the user on completion of the activity. The advantages and disadvantages of the use of the two different types of software to create TM activities will be discussed further in Chapter 4.

4

WHAT IS A 'DEDICATED PACKAGE'?

A dedicated package is software which sets up one or more TM activities, usually from text input by the teachers. For example, there are a number of gap filling authoring packages widely available such as *Gapmaster* from Wida*. These packages usually offer high quality presentation and a sophisticated range of authoring options which include the ability to:

- create gaps of varying lengths from parts of words to complete sentences;
- accept a number of different answers for the same gap;
- provide clues for each gap.

Packages such as *Fun with Texts* from Camsoft* offer a range of different activities based on the text input by the teacher, but do not always provide opportunities for the teacher to put in clues and appropriate feedback. *Fun with Texts* itself offers the following TM activities:

- sequencing of lines of text;
- gap filling and cloze tests;
- prediction;
- total and partial text reconstruction;
- decoding at word level;

INFOTECH
Text manipulation

- unscrambling at word level;

Dedicated packages are available with menu options and automatic feedback messages in English and in the major foreign languages taught in the UK.

Multiple choice (MC) software is not intrinsically concerned with text. However, in so far as it provides an environment in which gap fill activities can be set up, it deserves a mention. While most MC packages operate at sentence level, there is, of course, nothing to stop the author of an MC activity from breaking down a continuous text into chunks, each one of which is the subject of a multiple choice question of the gap fill kind. It is perhaps most useful, in TM terms, for encouraging recognition of either vocabulary or word forms. A multiple choice activity might be useful for students for whom word recognition is already a considerable achievement while those for whom word generation is a suitable challenge are required to generate their own input in a standard gap fill package.

TM AS A FORMAL ASSESSMENT ACTIVITY

5

Some very sophisticated packages exist which, while not designed specifically for use by language teachers and their students, accept accented characters and offer some elements of TM. The most widely used is *Question Mark** which has a gap filling option. Its sophistication lies in its ability to keep records of student input and scores, to print reports of this data and to export the data to spreadsheet applications for analysis. This approach is of potential interest to higher education institutions where continuous assessment of large numbers of students is a course requirement. However, the prime purpose of this book is the role of TM in fostering language learning and issues directly related to assessment will be not be covered here.

Previously Authored Packages

Sets of materials exist which contain ready-made TM activities which, in turn, require the purchase of the package in which they were authored. *Fun with Texts* is the most frequently used tool for the authoring of such sets of materials which are usually based on popular courses in the secondary sector. A number of different sets of materials are available from the publishers of *Fun with Texts* as well as from the publishers on whose courses the texts are based.

Multi-media TM

With the continued interest in TM software, software developers are beginning to update popular packages. *Gapkit* from Camsoft* is now available in a multimedia version, as is the collection of TM programs published by WIDA* as the 'Authoring Suite' which can also be purchased individually. All of these packages enable the teacher to include audio clips and graphics as part of the TM activity and, in the case of the WIDA packages, video clips.

6

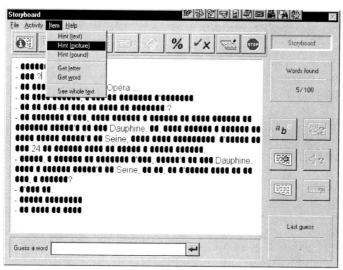

Text reconstruction with a picture clue in *Storyboard*
(*Storyboard* from Wida's *Authoring Suite*)

INFO TECH
Text manipulation

3 | What kind of language learning?

MODES OF LEARNING

TM in a computer classroom for a full or part class

TM software is flexible in terms of how it can be used. It is usually capable of being run on a network, although you should check out the requirements of multi-media versions of packages before purchase to ensure that your school network is capable of supporting them. Heavily used networks of a certain age might well make the distribution of audio and video files unacceptably slow for use by a whole class in the computer room.

7

If you find that you can run the TM software of your choice across your network, you should consider booking a computer room for all or part of your class on a regular basis. While pairs of students can work profitably together, it is usually acknowledged that groups of three students are better, particularly in primary and secondary classes. There are benefits to be gained from TM undertaken by groups of three students which are considered below in the section dealing with learning outcomes (p12).

In FE and HE, students who are working at a comparatively advanced level, or are experienced learners, tend to prefer working alone. However, when persuaded to try working with one or two other people, or when made to do so by force of circumstances, they often comment favourably on the learning opportunities which the arrangement offers, particularly if they are able to work entirely in the target language.

Group interaction is helped if students are allocated roles at the computer. For example, one student types in suggestions from the group, another student monitors the accuracy of what is typed in. A third student looks up words in the

dictionary and checks endings in the grammar reference book. The three students change roles every fifteen minutes or so, depending on the length of the lesson.

There is no reason why you should not take a full class into a computer room which does not have networked machines. However, under these circumstances, it is necessary to provide a disc for each computer which has been checked before use. It is then also important either that students know how to load software from disc, or that the teacher has enough time to go round each machine loading up the software before the class starts.

TM and the Internet

Tests created by the appropriate version of *Question Mark** are run satisfactorily across the Internet. They are used to enable teachers of distance learners to diagnose student weakness, and to enable the distance learners themselves to check their own progress.

There is a growing number of packages for Internet use which offer rudimentary text manipulation, usually confined to gapfilling, and with little if any diagnostic feedback. However, this is a growth area worth watching if you are in any way involved in teaching languages at a distance, or fancy setting homework which can be done on-line at home.

The most valuable role that the Internet can play in TM at the time of writing is that of a vast resource for texts on which to base activities. However, it should be noted that intellectual property rights exist on the Internet in the same way as they do with paper-based texts. Copyright restrictions do apply to WWW pages and should be respected. Useful starting points for locating suitable WWW texts are given in the Information section at the end of the book.

TM for small groups in the classroom

Some language teachers find it difficult to book time in the computer room, but have two or three computers in their classroom, which may or may not be networked. If the TM activities are well-integrated with other discrete activities, some of which do not depend on students having done the TM activity first, this arrangement works well. It works less well if the TM is provided as some kind of optional extra, with no real locus in the work of the class. Students tend to

8

INFO TECH
Text manipulation

have half an eye on computer availability and their concentration on the task in hand diminishes. When they get to the computer, the work that they do there is detached from their other work and lasting learning is unlikely to occur.

TM, a single computer, a projector and a full class

For school, college and university teachers lucky enough to have access to equipment which enables them to project the computer generated image on to a screen, the use of TM software with a whole class can provide an excellent environment in which to talk about language. It can also be useful for sharpening up both fluency and accuracy if the pace of the lesson is brisk.

FAVOURABLE CONDITIONS FOR LEARNING

Investigations into the characteristics of successful language learners (e.g. Stern, 1975; Naiman et al, 1978, reprinted 1996 and Rubin, 1981) suggest that good risk takers make good language learners. It is one thing to take a risk when there is the possibility of having another go if your first attempt fails, and another if you are to be judged on your first attempt. When students undertake a written assignment using ink on paper, the act has a degree of finality about it. The next time that they see the piece of paper, it is likely to have been 'marked' in a very literal sense. Most TM software allows students to edit their input before submitting it to the computer for 'marking'. This facility encourages students to have a go. The fact that the feedback can be instantaneous means that their thinking about the matter is not interrupted, as it is when they wait several days for the return of a paper-based exercise.

9

An additional spin-off from the ability to edit input is the way in which students tend to re-read the text many times when completing a TM activity. This frequent re-reading promotes subconscious language acquisition, while more conscious learning occurs as students consider the alternatives to proposed answers or to answers rejected by the computer.

Even when students are working in groups of three around a computer, their working environment is considerably less public than the classroom during a group or full class oral activity. This, allied with the anonymity of the computer, again tends to encourage students to 'have a go', to reflect on their errors and to keep trying until they get it right.

INFOTECH
Text manipulation

Most TM packages used in tutorial mode are designed to help students to 'get it right'. The activities are success-orientated, something which is not always easy to achieve in language teaching and learning. The fact that some of the TM activities are based on a games format also motivates learners and helps to keep them on task.

STAGES OF LEARNING

Teachers' views on the stages of language learning vary, as do the names which they give to these phases. In the context of this book, we will settle for the following stages:

10

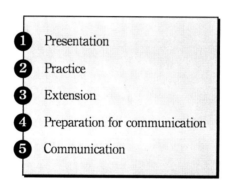

1. Presentation
2. Practice
3. Extension
4. Preparation for communication
5. Communication

By 'practice' I mean activities where students practise the new structure, vocabulary or skill within the same context in which it was initially presented to them. By 'extension', I mean activities in which the students practise their newly acquired language or skill in a new context. I see 'preparation for communication' as the stage at which students plan and undertake realistic tasks based on new and existing linguistic knowledge and skills in advance of incorporating them into a 'real life' communicative act.

TM software is of greatest use in phases 2 and 3, and has a valuable role to play in 4. It can be used to advantage in the Presentation phase in areas where a degree of 'discovery' learning is possible. You might, for example, take the view that vocabulary which is 'found' by students, rather than given to them, is more likely to be retained. If the new vocabulary is built into a text which they are required to reconstruct, they will need to infer from the context the likely

INFO TECH
Text manipulation

meaning of words that they do not yet know, look them up in the dictionary, take a decision about which word is best for the gap, try it out, and revisit the dictionary or ask for help if their informed guess does not prove to be correct.

The uses of TM in areas 2, 3 and 4 are fairly obvious and will be discussed in more detail in the section on learning outcomes below.

LEARNING STRATEGIES

In recent years interest has grown in the strategies which students use to accomplish the language learning tasks that we set them, and the strategies that some of them use to further their own learning.

As stated earlier, successful language learners tend to be good risk takers with a well developed ability to generate and test hypotheses and to revise their existing knowledge in the light of the outcomes. TM appears to encourage these behaviours in all students. It offers them the opportunity to take risks within a comparatively safe environment and to generate new responses following feedback from the computer about a previous incorrect attempt.

11

When used within well-designed tasks, TM software in general, and text reconstruction in particular, tend to promote the development and use of a wide range of language learning strategies. TM activities can be used to encourage students to make conscious use of the strategies if the students are given adequate preparation and the activities themselves require the use of the strategies. Issues related to task design will be addressed in subsequent chapters.

Language learning strategies are usually categorised as:

- **cognitive** when used to manipulate incoming information and to generate output in ways that enhance learning;

- **metacognitive** when used in the organisation of learning or task completion, involving planning how to tackle a learning activity, monitoring progress and evaluating success;

- **social/affective** when aspects of collaborative learning and interacting with others are involved to gain clarification, explanation or additional information.

When tasks which include TM activities are designed to involve students in collaborative work in which together they construct meaning or generate input, social and affective strategies are brought into play and the conditions for learning are often enhanced. Students are motivated, they remain on task, and they persevere. They are engaged in language processing and learning takes place.

Above all, well-set up TM activities will trigger the use of cognitive learning strategies, thus promoting successful language learning. The more the students need to process language, using the kind of strategies listed in Table 1 below, the more likely it is that linguistic knowledge will be committed to long-term memory and that 'deep' learning will take place.

Consideration will be given to the use of strategies in the discussion about task design in Chapter 5 (p38).

12 LEARNING OUTCOMES

The kind of learning that will take place with the use of TM software depends on the kind of TM used, and the way in which the task is designed. The potential is there to produce tasks in which, with the application of appropriate strategies, students are likely to:

- improve their knowledge of structure;
- improve their knowledge of form;
- apply and improve their knowledge of collocation;
- consolidate and improve their vocabulary;
- consolidate and improve their spelling and punctuation.

They will also have opportunities to:

- practise their reading, listening and writing skills;
- demonstrate understanding of information drawn from a source other than the TM text to use in the TM activity;
- gather information from the TM text for application elsewhere;
- develop a growing awareness of and ability to apply appropriate language learning strategies.

INFOTECH
Text manipulation

Metacognitive strategies	Cognitive strategies
Planning	**Predicting**
■ generating a plan for the accomplishment of a task ■ proposing strategies for the completion of a task ■ deciding to focus on certain aspects of a task ■ identifying problems to be overcome	■ using all available information including own world and linguistic knowledge to predict likely contents of text/gaps
Monitoring	**Inferring**
■ checking or correcting comprehension of 'incoming' text ■ checking or correcting input generated by self or partner(s) ■ monitoring progress in terms of plan and/or strategy use	■ using context to infer the meaning of missing words or chunks of text or the next chunk of text in a sequence
	Deducing
	■ using knowledge of rules to decide on the form of missing word(s) or the next word(s) in a sequence
Evaluating	**Resourcing**
■ of own or group's performance in terms of ability to complete the task ■ of own or group's L2 knowledge and/or use of language as a result of undertaking the task	■ seeking clarification and/or additional information and explanation including grammar hints and vocabulary from other students, teacher, grammar reference book or dictionary ■ creating own resource by note taking

Table 1: A summary of language learning strategies used in TM activities

13

They will also gain insights into the way in which texts are put together, for example, the links between tense markers and the formation of the tenses themselves, and into the differences in register if they are exposed to texts of varying styles and types.

14

INFO TECH

Text manipulation

4 Text manipulation activities

The following types of text manipulation are discussed in this chapter:

- sequencing;
- gap filling;
- cloze procedure;
- total or partial text reconstruction;
- unscrambling and decoding.

As was pointed in out in Chapter 2, there are substantial differences between TM activities set up in dedicated packages and those set up using a word processor. For this reason activities set up in a word processor will be discussed in a separate section at the end of this chapter (pp31–37).

For the most part, TM activities will form part of a wider task. However, in this chapter any mention of learning strategies and outcomes refer only to the TM activity itself. The kind of strategies and outcomes which can be anticipated in TM-related mixed skill tasks will be indicated in Chapter 5 (p38).

TM USING DEDICATED PACKAGES

Sequencing

This activity involves either matching pairs at phrase, sentence or short paragraph level, or re-ordering lines of text within a paragraph, but not within the same package. The relevant packages and their capabilities are listed in Table 2 (p18).

In the case of a continuous text, the length is usually limited to about eighteen lines. This enables the student to see the complete text and promotes the use of contextual clues since there is no need to scroll to see hidden sections of the text.

Sequencing software enables the author to type in texts of a length which the package can handle. The software itself then sets up the sequencing activity by jumbling the component parts and placing them in random order.

A word processor is the best tool with which to set up sequencing activities which involve the re-ordering of complete sentences within paragraphs and paragraphs within longer texts. This aspect of TM will be discussed in the section devoted to word processed applications at the end of this chapter (p31).

Sequencing software usually requires the student to click on the words or lines of text to be exchanged. Feedback is limited to acceptance of a correct attempt at positioning, and rejection of an incorrect attempt. Students tend not to find this frustrating, but rise to the challenge and consider alternatives. As even continuous texts do not usually exceed eighteen lines in length, it is always possible for students to complete this activity successfully, something which they find motivating.

16

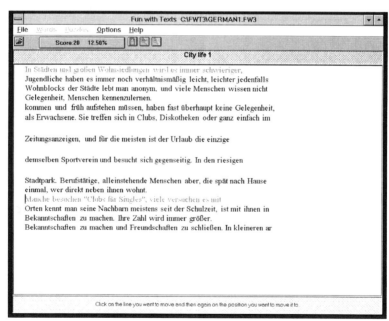

Sequencing in *Fun with Texts*
(Textsalad from Camsoft's *Fun with Texts 3*)

As with all TM activities, the stimulus for a sequencing activity is quite likely to arise from a source other than the text itself. Examples are given in the mini-case studies below.

Strategy use

In completing TM activities, students are likely to bring into play aspects of the major metacognitive strategies of monitoring and evaluating as well as engaging in predicting, inferring, deducing and, to a lesser extent, resourcing.

In appropriately set up activities they are likely to improve their knowledge of structure, form and collocation. In the case of the re-ordering of lines within a paragraph, they will also practise the kind of reading skills necessary to establish gist and detailed meaning through an appreciation of the inter-relationships of ideas within the text and the devices used by the author to establish them.

17

Mini-case study 1

A group of young learners in the primary sector have been introduced to the names of buildings in a town and to directions. Their teacher wants to give them practice in following directions. She has typed in a set of directions based on a town plan. The software jumbles the text, line by line. The students put the lines into the correct order, using the knowledge acquired earlier and with the help of the plan. They predict line order based on incoming information and deduce order from their knowledge of the structures and vocabulary used in the text. Their final job is to identify the location of the entrance to a secret tunnel to which the directions lead them.

Mini-case study 2

Some GNVQ students have been set the task of summarising the contents of a tourist leaflet in English for intending visitors from Germany. In order to help them to undertake this task, their teacher has provided them with a similar leaflet and a summary in jumbled form. They have discussed the main points of this leaflet with their teacher and made notes to help them with the sequencing activity. When they have unjumbled the text, they go on to reconstruct it before noting down any useful link words and phrases which they can use in their own summary.

18

Major packages available	Student interaction	Mode of use	Strategy use	Learning outcomes
Matchmaster	Pressing appropriate buttons	Individual, small groups or whole class	Monitoring	Structure
			Evaluating	Form
Fun with Texts (Text Salad)	Highlighting text, and pressing the Enter key	Self- access or teacher led	Predicting	Collocation
			Inferring	Reading skills
			Deducing	

Table 2: Summary of sequencing software

INFO TECH

Text manipulation

Gap filling

The most frequently used TM activity, whether on paper or on computer, remains gap filling. Most modern dedicated packages enable teachers to input a text of several screen's length and to insert gaps wherever they feel it relevant to do so. Indeed, they can take the same text and vary the number and types of gaps to meet the differing needs of their students, or to provide extension activities for quick workers. It is also useful to remember that word endings and phrases can be gapped as well as single words. The ability to vary the length of the gaps means that the author of the activity is free to set the learning outcomes which can cover the whole range of those listed in the previous chapter. However, make certain when you create the gaps that the student has adequate prior knowledge to be able to infer the likely contents of the gap and/or that the immediate context is enough to enable them to infer the contents. You should also ensure that students have the prior knowledge to enable them to deduce the correct form of the words to fill the gaps.

As well as the skill required by the author to identify appropriate gaps, there is a great deal of skill in writing clues and feedback to incorrect answers for packages which offer these facilities. The skill does not lie in making the technology work. That is usually easy. What is difficult is to resist the temptation to provide comments which lead students quickly and easily to the 'answer' without having to do much thinking for themselves. They will retain much more if they have to work for it than if they are handed an answer on a plate. A clue, whether it is provided before input or after erroneous input, should be a trigger to further thought, not a fast track to the answer. Some packages provide in-built clues. For example, if a student types in '*sprechen*' when the answer is '*spreche*' they might be told that they have typed too many letters. On the other hand, if they type in '*spreche*' instead of '*Sprache*', their answer will remain, but there will be a gap at the point where there is a mistake in the spelling.

In the majority of gap fill and cloze test packages students are required to identify the gap that they are targetting and to type in the word or words which they believe are missing. Accuracy of spelling is required. Feedback can be simply 'Correct' or 'Incorrect' if the software is operating in 'test' mode. If it is set to run in 'tutorial' mode, feedback will be given on incorrect answers in the form of clues which have either been created by the teacher/author or which are supplied by the software by indicating to students those letters of their input which are correct.

19

```
Gapmaster: Reitschule                                                    ⬜
File  Activity  Item  Help

  [ℹ]  [⬛]  [ ]  [ ]  [ ]  [◆]  [%]  [✓✗]  [⬛]  [STOP]    [ Exploratory mode ]

 ┌─────────────────────────────────────────────┐  ┌──────────────────┐
 │Also, hier in der Café Reitschule, also wir sind ein sehr großes ? hier,│  │  Gap   2         │
 │weil das Café hat über 300 sitzen und wir ham 19 Stunden am Tag│  │                  │
 │offen, jeden Tag, wir haben keinen Ruhetag, und  wir sind also│  │  [⬛]    [⬛]      │
 │insgesamt hier vier                            │  │                  │
 │? und wir haben über vierzig ?, zehn ? und ? zehn Leute und ungefähr│  │                  │
 │zwanzig Leute, die  ?  arbeiten, und, das ist zum Teil sehr│  │  [⬛]    [a⬛]     │
 │anstrengend, weil man so viele viele ? hat, mit denen man ständig│  │                  │
 │reden muß , es passieren Fehler, natürlich, ein Fehler ist nicht so│  │  [◀?]   [⬛]      │
 │schlimm, aber bei 40 Leuten jeden Tag, jeden Tag das gleiche, das│  │                  │
 │ist schon anstrengend.                         │  └──────────────────┘
 └─────────────────────────────────────────────┘   [ Sound hint ]

  [✗]  [ sitzen                          ]  [↵]          [  ↑  ]
  [⬛]  ●itz●●●●●●                                        [  ↑  ]
  [⬛]  Das Gegenteil von Stehplätze                      [  ↓  ]
                                                          [  ±  ]
```

**Feedback in
Gapmaster**

(Gapmaster from
Wida's *Authoring
Suite*)

20

Cloze tests

Cloze tests are a specific kind of gap fill activity in which the whole or part of every 'n'th word is deleted. When paper-based they tend to be tests and nothing more. However, when computer-based they become a much more flexible tool since the user can vary the frequency of the gaps and work through the text several times at different levels of difficulty. This frequent exposure to the text reinforces the structures within the text as well as repeatedly drawing the learner's attention to the gapped words. It is not possible to have clues in cloze tests because of the variability of the gaps. Test scores are usually given to the student but are not retained on disc.

Strategy use

Students are likely to utilise the full range of metacognitive and cognitive strategies listed in the previous chapter. However, in the case of cognitive strategies, the emphasis placed on each strategy will vary according to the focus of the gaps. It would be possible, for example, to set up two versions of a text. In the first version key words of the main theme(s) of the text could be gapped and students provided with a list of ten possible words from which to choose three. They would be encouraged to predict content and skim the text in order to identify and place correctly three of the ten given

INFO TECH
Text manipulation

words. In a second version of the text, words which conveyed detailed information could be gapped and students provided with a set of questions to which they have to find answers within the text. As a result of a close reading of the text in order to find answers to the questions, they would be able to predict the class of the missing words and try out their hunches as to the word itself and the correct form, given the context and their knowledge of the relevant rule(s).

This might sound like a very complicated way of getting students to fill in a few gaps. However, by creating a problem for them to solve which includes both information gap and information transfer, you will be creating an activity which will raise the students' cognitive activity and which will enable them to consolidate knowledge, thereby improving both their fluency and accuracy.

Mini-case study 3

A group of first year degree students who are following an intensive ab initio course in Spanish have been taught the forms of the preterite and imperfect tenses in their weekly grammar classes. They have a weekly session in the computer lab as a follow-up to these classes. Their teacher has set up a text in which all the verbs have been replaced by gaps. The text is a third person version of a text which the students have previously read in form of a first person account of their plans for the weekend ahead in which, for the most part, they have used '*ir*' + infinitive to express their intentions and the simple present to express what they usually do.

21

Mini-case study 4

A group of post-16 students of French are anxious to improve their ability to spell words which they hear but do not see, to enable them to make a note of them and look them up in a dictionary. Their teacher has put together a text which contains a significant number of words which are difficult to spell, and a number of verbs with silent endings or irregular forms. The teacher has recorded the text as a series of separate sentences. In the first version of the gapped text, words which are difficult to spell are gapped. In the second version it is the turn of the verbs. The students are required to produce a list of the infinitives of the gapped verbs and their meanings. They can hear the audio clips or watch the sentences as often as they like by clicking on an icon in the text.

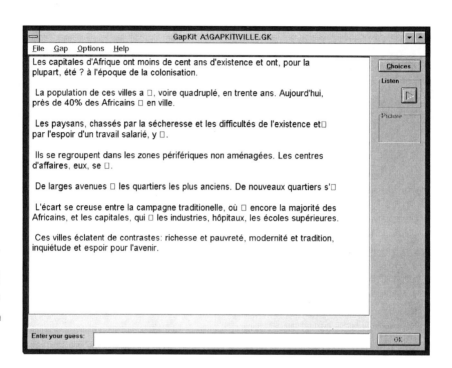

**Click on the 'Listen' button to hear a recording
of the sentence which contains the gap**
(*Multimedia Gapkit* from Camsoft)

INFOTECH
Text manipulation

Major packages available	Student interaction	Mode of use	Strategy use	Learning outcomes
Gapkit *Gapmaster* *Fun with Texts* (Cloze)	Typing in words	Individual, small groups or whole class	Planning Monitoring Evaluating Predicting Inferring Deducing Resourcing	Structure Form Collocation Vocabulary Reading skills Spelling
Choicemaster	Selecting words	Self- access or teacher led		

Table 3: Summary of gap fill software including MC and cloze tests

23

Total and partial text reconstruction

The most extreme form of gap filling is total text reconstruction. In this form of text manipulation the student is faced with a screen in which the letters of every word have been replaced by a character such as an asterisk or a dash. Their job is to type in a word which they think is in the text. Their prediction is likely to be based on their knowledge of the text type, previous stimulus materials and on any support materials available to them during the TM activity. When students type in a word which is in the text, every occurrence then appears. This is always an encouraging event.

As the text builds up, contextual clues become available and students begin to infer and deduce what is missing. When they find themselves defeated by a gap, they can ask their teacher for help, look up words in a dictionary, or check things such as verb forms in a grammar reference book. They can also turn to the 'help' facilities, an action which tends to result in a loss of points.

24

This kind of software usually offers the option of seeing the text before making a start on the activity. If students are allowed frequently to take up this option, they are unlikely to derive the maximum benefit from the activity since it will tend to become an exercise based on short-term memory, rather than an exercise designed to promote intense cognitive activity and, therefore, deep learning.

The only feedback given for an incorrect 'guess' is an indication that the word is not in the text, which might sound unhelpful. That might well be so if the aim is to complete the text as quickly as possible. However, it is very helpful in terms of forcing students to examine their original hypothesis, revise it and try again. As mentioned above, if all else fails, help is available. Students can request letters and words, or even have a brief look at the full text, but it will cause points to be knocked off their score. Despite its daunting appearance, this activity is success-orientated. It does not take long for students to recognise this and the fact that it has a gaming element to it. They see themselves as competing against the computer. They recognise the machine's limitations and are rarely upset if a seemingly correct entry is rejected. They set out on a text reconstruction activity confidently and with the expectation of success. That cannot always be the case when they are required to generate input without immediate feedback, either by computer or with a pen.

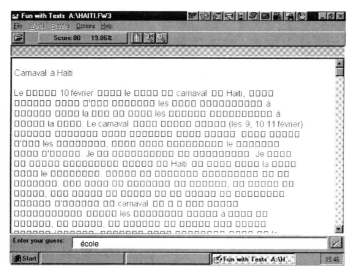

Text reconstruction in *Fun with Texts*
(Copywrite (Hard) from Camsoft's *Fun with Texts 3*)

25

In most packages of this kind it is now possible for authors to leave in words of their choice which they feel essential for the completion of the task. Such words might include proper nouns. It is also usual for numbers expressed as figures to be retained.

Because of the opportunity given to an author to retain as many words as he or she wishes, it is a simple matter to produce exercises of varying levels of difficulty based on the same text by saving under separate names versions with differing numbers and types of words retained.

Text reconstruction provides a rich learning environment within which students constantly re-read text and engage intensively in high level cognitive activity. In particular, they engage in frequent hypothesis formulation and revision and apply their own linguistic knowledge and the information gained from the emerging text to the resolution of the problems set by the software. It is not unusual for students to take well in excess of 60 linguistic decisions during a half-hour text reconstruction session (Hewer, 1993), and teachers report long-term retention of vocabulary and grammar practised in text reconstruction activities.

INFOTECH
Text manipulation

When text reconstruction is undertaken in a pair or group of three, discussion around the computer is inevitably in the students' mother tongue in a monoglot class. In a polyglot class use of the target language is more likely, especially with advanced students, but by no means certain. Teachers have to decide whether or not the perceived gains arising from the use of the software outweigh a departure from the use of the target language, if that is their usual practice.

Software is available for a different kind of text reconstruction which is, in effect, multiple choice. Students are confronted with a blank screen and a list of words, phrases or sentences from which they have to select the correct initial word. A further list is then displayed and a choice made from it. In this way the entire text is reconstructed. The critical difference between this kind of text reconstruction and that described above is that this kind is essentially a recognition exercise, while students have to generate their own words to input in the activity described in the previous section. It is likely that the generation of input makes an important contribution to the learning process and that this is the reason why text reconstruction is held in high esteem by students and teachers alike and has been so since its first appearance during the early eighties.

26

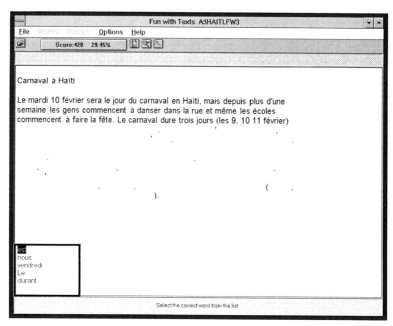

Prediction in *Fun with Texts*
(Predict from Camsoft's *Fun with Texts 3*)

Text manipulation

Text reconstruction software enables the author of the activity to:

- input text, usually of about eighteen lines;
- retain selected words.

Mini-case study 5

A group of young learners of Spanish in their last year at primary school have studied the vocabulary and structures necessary to read about their link class's school and to describe their own. The link classes correspond by e-mail as well as by traditional mail. The link class has sent a set of photographs of their school and has e-mailed a short description, in simple Spanish, as requested by their teacher. The teacher has read out the e-mail to the class at the same time as she showed them the relevant photographs. The teacher has fed the incoming e-mail into the text reconstruction package and the children take it in turns to go to the classroom computer in groups of three to reconstruct the text. The photos have been labelled and pinned up by the computer to help them. As a follow up to this activity they will have the opportunity of editing the incoming e-mail to make it fit their school, having had a full class discussion about this with their teacher.

27

Mini-case study 6

A group of FE students studying French for vocational purposes have been asked to give a presentation of the financial profile of their company to potential investors. They have the necessary information in the form of bar charts. They have spent some time interpreting the charts and gathering together the necessary vocabulary and structures that they feel they will need in order to draft their presentation. Their teacher has provided them with an additional set of bar charts relating to another company and has input into the *Fun with Texts* package a text summarising the financial position of this company as revealed by the charts. The students first build up the text word by word using the multiple choice option described above. They then turn to the total text reconstruction component and use the knowledge that they have acquired before to predict, infer and deduce missing words. In the light of this work, they revise their notes of useful structures and go on to develop their own summary using a word processor.

Major packages available	Student interaction	Mode of use	Strategy use	Learning outcomes
Storyboard *Fun with Texts* (Copywrite Hard and Easy) *Eclipse*	Typing in words	Individual, small groups or whole class	Planning Monitoring Evaluating Predicting Inferring Deducing Resourcing	Structure Form Collocation Vocabulary Reading skills Spelling
Fun with Texts (Predict) *Sequitur*	Selecting words	Self-access or teacher led		Structure Form Vocabulary Reading skills

Table 4: Text reconstruction software

INFOTECH

Text manipulation

Unscrambling and decoding words

There is no doubt that younger learners enjoy these two activities. They are currently only widely available in *Fun with Texts*. Using the text input by the author of the activity, the software either scrambles the letters within each word of the text, or codes the text by, for example, replacing every occurrence of the letter 'o' by 'j'.

The students' task is to either unscramble the words by typing in what they believe to be the correct spelling of the word, or to crack the code by typing in a letter, followed by the letter they believe that it represents. Feedback is similar to that found in the sequencing and text reconstruction components of *Fun with Texts*. Correct input is accepted and incorrect input is rejected. No clues are given.

In working through a text at letter level, it is likely that students will tend to focus on the spelling of individual words, turning to their possible meaning within a wider context when they get stuck. This approach will limit the range of strategies that they use and will probably, as a result, diminish the lasting learning that takes place, although students will have to use both deduction and inferencing to succeed, particularly in the decoding option.

29

Some students will find the 'unscrambling' activity tedious because every word in the text has to be unjumbled. However, the decoding activity contains more surprises for the student in that once the code for a letter has been cracked, all occurrences of the letter in the text will be changed. This raises student motivation and increases their enjoyment.

If pleasure is gained from these two activities and you feel that students will benefit from working through them, it is probably useful to keep them in reserve as follow-on activities for fast workers when you have a full class with a wide ability range in the computer room.

There are no additional requirements for setting this activity up in *Fun with Texts* other than the typing in of the source text. The computer does the rest.

Given that these activities operate at word level and are perhaps of lesser value than other TM activities in supporting learning, it is possibly not the best use of students' time to base a task on this activity, except, perhaps, as an occasional treat for younger learners as part of an international 'whodunnit' project.

INFOTECH
Text manipulation

Major packages available	Student interaction	Mode of use	Strategy use	Learning outcomes
Fun with Texts (Scrambler and Enigma)	Typing in words or letters	Individual, small groups or whole class Self-access or teacher led	Planning Monitoring Evaluating Inferring Deducing Resourcing	Form Vocabulary Spelling

Table 5: Unscrambling and decoding software

INFO TECH

Text manipulation

TM USING A WORD PROCESSOR

Because the computer can provide immediate feedback and automatic scoring, we tend to overlook the potential of the word processor as a tool for setting up computer-based language learning activities because of the lack of those facilities. This is a pity since its extreme flexibility enables it to provide not only some of the activities described above, but also activities impossible to set up within widely available dedicated packages. You might still have to provide the feedback and/or to mark the results, but at least, unlike some hand-written offerings, they will be clearly legible!

The use of a word processor in language learning gives students the opportunity to apply and develop transferable skills likely to be of life-long value in both personal and vocational terms.

A word processor enables the user to:

- insert and delete words;
- move chunks of text around within a document using the copy/cut and paste option;
- search a document for occurrences of a given word or phrase and to replace it automatically.

31

These facilities enable teachers to set up sequencing and gap filling. It is not possible, however, to set up total and partial text reconstruction or decoding activities because instant feedback is a necessary part of the procedure. The lack of feedback might well result in less intensive cognitive strategy use during sequencing and gap filling activities, but might improve the ability of students to monitor and evaluate their own performance. Lack of feedback might also diminish motivation. These two factors suggest that in a straight choice between a sequencing or gap fill exercise using a dedicated package and the same exercise using a word processor, the dedicated package would be the better choice. However, as indicated above, you will not always be comparing like with like. In some instances the word processor, because of its great flexibility, will be the better tool for the job. This will be the case with variations on the types of sequencing provided by dedicated packages, with gap filling designed to promote as wide a range as possible of words to fill the gaps, and with more creative activities which it is not possible to set up using a dedicated package. This creative kind of text manipulation involves text expansion,

INFOTECH
Text manipulation

contraction and transformation which can provide excellent preparation for subsequent, freer writing.

The scrambling of letters within words is not a sensible thing to try to do within a word processor. Without feedback, the potential for the activity to degenerate swiftly into chaos is considerable!

Sequencing

The copy/cut and paste options make the word processor an appropriate tool for setting up sequencing activities. Because of the flexibility which it offers, it is you, rather than the computer program, who decides on the unit of text to be moved around. You can, therefore, set up sequencing activities at word, sentence and paragraph level without difficulty and can vary the difficulty of activities set up using the same task by varying the length of unit on which you base the activity. Some students might find it easier to make a start with meaningful chunks of two or three sentences, while others might enjoy the increased challenge of re-ordering single sentences.

32

Without automatic feedback, students will not be forced to reconsider their decisions. They will need to be reminded to check their work thoroughly, perhaps by reading aloud the results of their work to see if it 'sounds right'. They will need to engage in self-motivated self-monitoring and evaluation, which is something to be encouraged. If you are present at the time when your students work on the activity, you can provide feedback for them. Make certain that the feedback that you give them is designed to force them into further cognitive activity, and not designed simply to enable them to complete the task. We know that students like to have 'products'. We are sometimes guilty of seeing task completion as a desirable end in itself, without always considering the relevance to student learning of the means by which completion was achieved. Try pointing out errors to students and, possibly, giving them some idea about the nature of the error. Avoid giving them the correction in mid-task.

If you are planning on marking the students' work, you will need to ensure that it is possible for them either to print off their work in good time before the end of the class, or to save it in a location where you will both be able to find it and to identify whose work it is.

Whether your students are working in self-access mode, or in a class at which you are present, you might want them to correct their own work. Corrections on

paper rarely get done and students miss out on the learning opportunities which error correction provides. However, error correction on computer is much more motivating for students because they end up with a perfect product, and satisfying for teachers because errors become a stepping stone to success, rather than a mark of failure. You can always provide access to a file containing the correct version of the text that you have had your students re-order. If the work is being done in a taught class, you can give students the relevant file name when you feel that it is appropriate to do so. You might, for example, discuss with them the results of their first attempt at re-ordering and ask them to review the sequence at certain points before making the correction available to them.

It is simple enough, then, to set up sequencing activities in a word processor. You can either type in a text, or use an incoming e-mail message, or a text from a WWW site. Once you have got an error-free copy of the source text, save it. Now decide on the level at which you plan to set up your 'jumble'. Cut and paste the units of text in a way which will present a challenge to your students, leaving at least one blank line between each unit of text. Some people like to number the units of text. Younger learners find this helpful, particularly if the text is longer than can be seen on a single screen in its entirety. Remember to insert any necessary instructions regarding the activity, or the task within which it is set, at the top of the file. Students might need to be reminded about where and under what name to save their version of the text if that is what is required. It can be helpful to put instructions in italics to differentiate them from the text. When you are happy that the instructions are clear and that the whole text is present, albeit in jumbled order, save the file under a different name from the one which you used for the correct version.

33

Mini-case study 7

A secondary class in their first year of Spanish have spent some time learning how to tell the time, mainly through listening and speaking activities. Their teacher wants to give them practice in recognising the written forms. The teacher has created a text which follows the daily routine of a young person in Spain. The text on which the students will work has the activities in the wrong order. The text is based on an audio recording from the course in use. The students have already heard the recording several times. It is possible for them to click on an icon and hear a recording of the text from within the word processed document. The students, working in groups of three in the multi-media computer room, have a worksheet with them on which the times, in the correct sequence, are shown. Their job is to get the text into the correct sequence, print off a copy of their version, check it with their teacher and, in a subsequent lesson, to fill in the details about what the Spanish student does at each of the times given.

34

Gap fill activities

Clearly it is simple enough to create gaps in texts using a word processor. However, it is worth giving some thought to the way in which you plan to present the activity, taking into account how difficult you want to make it, and the ways in which students are likely to tackle it.

Your gaps can consist of parts of words, whole words, phrases or, in extreme cases, sentences. In some gaps there will only be one correct answer. In other gaps you might be prepared to accept a range of answers. Indeed, you might be using the activity to encourage diversity of response as a vocabulary building exercise. You might want to indicate the likely content of the gap by replacing the letters with the correct number of dashes or asterisks, and/or by giving the first letter of each word. You might want to provide several versions of the activity at different levels of difficulty. One version could contain a list of the gapped words at the bottom of the text which students could then cut and paste into position to avoid having to type them in.

Whatever decisions you take about the nature and appearance of the gaps, it is advisable to indicate where they begin and end, preferably by putting an asterisk at the beginning and end of each gap which students should not delete. If you insert asterisks, students will know where the gaps are if they decide to change one or more of their responses. You and/or they will know where the

gaps are when they come to correct their work. In the source text you should put number and asterisks before and after the word to be gapped in order to make correction easy either for yourself or for students. Remember to name files carefully so that you can recognise from the file name which is the source text and at what level of difficulty the different versions of the activity itself are. You might also like to print out your files, along with any relevant documentation, and maintain a paper file for quick reference when away from the computer. It is good departmental policy to maintain such files to avoid duplication of effort.

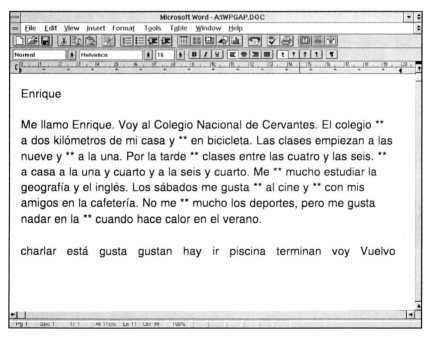

35

Enrique

Me llamo Enrique. Voy al Colegio Nacional de Cervantes. El colegio ** a dos kilómetros de mi casa y ** en bicicleta. Las clases empiezan a las nueve y ** a la una. Por la tarde ** clases entre las cuatro y las seis. ** a casa a la una y cuarto y a la seis y cuarto. Me ** mucho estudiar la geografía y el inglés. Los sábados me gusta ** al cine y ** con mis amigos en la cafetería. No me ** mucho los deportes, pero me gusta nadar en la ** cuando hace calor en el verano.

charlar   está   gusta   gustan   hay   ir   piscina   terminan   voy   Vuelvo

Gapfilling using a word processed file

36

Mini-case study 8

The teacher of a bottom set of third year secondary students of French is working on their reading skills. She has no TM software available, but does have access to enough networked computers to enable her to let the students work in pairs on a word processed gap fill activity. The purpose of the activity is to help the students to improve their skimming and scanning skills. The teacher has taken the text of an article about a school in a Francophone country, taken from a **WWW** page, and saved it. She has gapped four words related to the main points in the text, which she has placed in random order at the bottom of the text. She has marked the gaps by two asterisks, but has not given any indication of the length of each gap. She has saved this file. She has loaded in the original text again and has removed the key words in six sentences which carry answers to questions which the students have to answer when they have filled the gaps. The questions contain clues to the words in the gaps. She has made a list of the gapped words in one version of the text but has not done so in the other. This will enable her to challenge the quicker workers to produce the words for themselves when they have completed the 'cut and paste' version.

Text expansion, contraction and transformation

These techniques can be used to set up a wide range of activities such as:

- adding adjectives or adverbs to a text to make it more interesting;
- completion of sentences within a text in order to maintain the narrative;
- adding a 'middle' to a text for which the beginning and end have been provided;
- replacing details in a text in order to personalise it;
- replacing details in a text in order to make it fit a photograph, diagram or plan;
- cutting down and editing a text to restrict it to the main points;
- transforming a text so that it becomes reported speech;
- transforming a text so that it becomes a past report rather than a future plan;
- editing a text in response to incoming information from an audio or video text.

INFO TECH

Text manipulation

Mini-case study 9

A group of post-16 German specialists in their second term of an Advanced level course are aware that they are experiencing difficulties in developing their writing skills, especially their ability to write complex and compound sentences. In order to help them, their teacher has put together a text containing only simple sentences. They have read the text together and talked about the kind of impression that it gives to the reader in its present form. During their free time they have worked either as individuals, or with a partner, to insert and delete words in the text to form compound and complex sentences in order to make the text more readable, to clarify relationships within the text, and to make it sound as if it was written by someone of some maturity. When everyone has completed the task and handed in a printout of their work, the group considers the various versions and decides on which one they prefer, and why.

The choice of activity and the way in which you set it up will depend entirely on the kind of learning that you hope it will promote. As with TM activities set up using a dedicated package, those which involve some form of information gap and/or information transfer are more likely to provoke frequent strategy use of the kind which promotes lasting learning.

37

It is possible to do limited forms of text expansion and transformation using the Wida* software *Testmaster* package which will also enable you to provide feedback. Questions can have up to four correct answers ranging from single words to complete sentences. Your choice of tool depends on your purpose for setting up the activity. For example, if you want to give practice in or test sentence joining techniques in an exercise in which there is a limited range of correct answers, *Testmaster* would be a good choice. If, on the other hand, you wanted to provide students with the opportunity to use as wide a range of vocabulary as possible in order to make a narrative interesting but plausible, a word processor would be the appropriate choice. An activity like this can lead on to a classroom competition to decide on the best story 'published' by members of the group, based on the original framework provided by the teacher.

When you set up activities in the word processor such as the ones listed on the previous pages, the important thing to remember is to give crystal clear instructions and to make certain that students understand that, if they contrive to mess up the 'framework' text, they can always load it again and make a fresh start.

5 Task-based text manipulation

Up to this point in the book we have considered TM activities in their own right, rather than as components of a broader language learning task. There are many occasions when it is entirely appropriate to use such activities as independent exercises provided that they are fully integrated with other course activities. For example, TM activities provide useful practice opportunities for a single student in self-access mode who wishes to focus on a particular grammar point or topic area. However, they bring added value to the usual range of activities when they are included as integral components of a mixed skill task.

This chapter deals with the principles and stages involved in task design where there is a TM component. It is set against the background of a belief that computer-based language learning activities of any kind are only likely to lead to learning if they are:

- of clear relevance to the course in the eyes of the student;
- fully integrated with other activities;

and if they ensure that students:

- engage with the target language rather than merely observe it;
- are provoked into the use of language learning strategies likely to lead to increased internal cognitive activity;
- are given the opportunity to consolidate and/or expand their existing knowledge of the language and how to use it appropriately and correctly.

This is a tall order, especially if we take into account the fact that language learners' needs differ, whether they are working alone on a task or collaborating with others.

It is helpful to have a framework within which to design a task. It is important, however, not to get so involved in filling in the framework that the reality of the learners and the practicalities of classroom implementation are forgotten. The following are suggested components of the framework. Although produced here in linear order, they are inevitably inter-related and it is often difficult to complete one stage without reference to at least one other.

1 Identify the needs of your students in the context of the course

2 Define the learning objectives of the task

3 Define the assessment

4 Identify all available source materials and media

5 Plan the component learning activities indicating the medium to be used for each

6 Create and/or identify the learning and/or support materials including guidance on strategy use

7 Implement the activities

8 Carry out the assessment

9 Evaluate the task

10 Revise

39

Despite appearances, what is suggested here is not something akin to writing a mini course book! It is simply a method for developing systematically a series of linked activities and combining them into a task which has a number of short- and longer-term goals for students to aim for as they progress through the various stages.

What follows is a task set for teenage intermediate learners starting their fifth year of studying French at secondary level, at the end of which they will take a public examination for which they are expected to produce three pieces of course

work written in French. The task is designed to be completed over a four-week period. The teacher will provide input about the target verb forms.

❶ Identify the needs of your students in the context of the course

The students for whom the task has been designed are high-fliers and know that they have to be able to refer to past, present and future events and to express personal opinions if they want to get one of the three top grades. Their teacher has decided to revise thoroughly the forms of the various tenses during the first term of their fifth year and to make a start with the simple future and the future with '*aller*'. The teacher and the students have taken a joint decision to base the first task on a topic related to the world of work, one of the three topics for which they plan to produce a coursework assignment for assessment. For the most part the students will work in groups of three, although there are aspects of the task which will require them to work individually. Each group will be paired with another group for the exchange of advertisements and the interviews which will be conducted towards the end of the task.

40

❷ Define the learning objectives of the task

The objectives of the task in terms of language learning are to provide the opportunity for the students to:

- revise the form and uses of the simple future tense and the future with '*aller*' both in terms of recognition and production;

- extend their vocabulary to cover a number of job titles and the kind of activities associated with the jobs;

- extend their vocabulary to enable them to talk and write about conditions of work (number of hours, holidays, etc);

- build up their knowledge of ways in which to express their opinion about why a certain job would suit them and begin to make active use of this knowledge.

INFO TECH
Text manipulation

❸ Define the assessment

The final component of the task is the production of a paragraph in a letter (200 words approximately) to a friend in which individual students identify an imaginary summer job or part-time job that they are going to do, what their duties are going to be and why they feel that they are well suited to do the job.

❹ Identify all available source materials and media

The teacher has already gathered together a number of newspaper advertisements for jobs to provide a starting point for the vocabulary of job titles. He or she has also found the address of a WWW page which lists job vacancies. He or she has decided to use an audio clip of a job interview from a published course as a resource. As part of the forward planning for the activity at the end of the previous year, the class collaborated to plan, draft, revise and send an e-mail message to their link class requesting messages about the jobs that the French students wanted to do when they left school and why they thought they would be good at them.

41

Audio cassette players with listening facilities for up to three students are available in the classroom.

The school has a networked computer room for use by all departments via a booking system. The teacher has booked the room for one 50-minute lesson each week for the first two weeks of the four-week period allocated for completion of the task. There is also a networked computer with Internet access and a local printer in the classroom which students can request to use during and outside class time on the basis of need.

❺ Plan the component learning activities indicating the medium to be used for each

The task requires the students, working in groups of three, to:

- produce an advertisement for a job which they would find attractive;

- conduct an interview with three candidates (from another group) for the job during which they explain what the candidate will do if appointed and to be candidates for a job advertised by their paired group;

- ask the candidate to explain why they think they are suited to the job.

Task-based text manipulation

Preparatory work is necessary to enable the students to meet the above requirements by helping them to learn thoroughly and retain the vocabulary and structures associated with the topic. The TM activities are designed specifically to provide the necessary consolidation and practice for this to happen, following the teacher's input.

The task has eight sub-tasks which are as follows:

A **Reading job advertisements, six comprehension questions and note taking + WWW activity searching for five vacancies in particular job areas**

Students to be encouraged to use own world knowledge and look up words in a dictionary for meaning and to check the spelling.

B **Gap filling and text reconstruction activities**

Text of job advertisement for the gap fill to be created based on those used in A. Text for text reconstruction to be created based on a written description of the duties and conditions of service of the job advertised in the gap fill activity.

Students to be advised to make use of context in the gap fill and to plan their approach to the text reconstruction task before making a start. Once started, they are advised to make full use of the emerging context and also to try to identify the reason why any words are rejected by the computer by considering the appropriateness of the word tried, and also its form.

C **Listening activity**

Use audio clip of job interview from course book. Write five comprehension questions. Indicate that students should expect to hear some of the vocabulary that they encountered during the two previous stages.

Students to be advised to listen out for specific key words to help them to locate the sections of the clip that they have to answer question on about the duties of the job and the conditions of service. They are also given key words to listen for to lead them to the identification of structures which they will find useful in saying why they think that they are well suited for a job. They are asked to note down useful structures.

42

INFOTECH
Text manipulation

D Sequencing and two text reconstruction activities

Text for the sequencing activity and the first text reconstruction activity to be selected from the incoming e-mail messages from the link school and second text created for second text reconstruction activity, based on the section of the audio clip where the candidate talks about why he or she is well suited for the job and what he or she will enjoy about it.

Students are advised to apply their knowledge of sentence structure and form during the sequencing activity. During the first text reconstruction activity they are encouraged to work quickly, brainstorming the text for words remembered from the sequencing activity, but paying attention to the accuracy of the words that they type in. During the second text reconstruction activity they are encouraged to look back to the notes that they made during the listening activity as well as to base their prediction of missing words on the contents of the emerging text.

E Creation by group of an advertisement plus writing of notes by group to enable them to talk about what the successful candidate will do when in post and generation of up to three questions to ask each candidate during the interview. Advertisements exchanged between paired groups.

43

Students to be encouraged to plan the content of their advertisement carefully before beginning to write it, and to look again at the advertisements which they worked on during Stage 1 to get ideas. Students also encouraged to work out the key words and structures necessary to say what the successful candidate will do when in post.

F Individual students plan what they will say when asked during the interview in G why they are suited to the job advertised by their paired group

Students to be encouraged to plan carefully what they will say, to identify the key words and structures, to make notes and to practise their answer. Warn them that they will not be able to read their answer out, nor to take their notes into the interview.

G One group interviews the members of the paired group and then the groups change roles

Students are advised to make notes of the answers given by each of the candidates to enable them to compare the responses when they come to decide who to offer the job to.

INFOTECH
Text manipulation

H Working as individuals on the previously defined assessment, **the students compose a paragraph of a letter to a friend** in which they name an imaginary holiday or part-time job that they are going to do, or a full-time job that they imagine themselves doing. They list the kind of things it will involve them in doing and why they think that they will be good at it and enjoy doing it. Instructions for this to be written.

❻ *Create and/or identify the learning and/or support material including guidance on strategy use*

The teacher creates the worksheets for the reading and listening tasks using the word processing package on the classroom computer and prints off enough copies for each group. He or she also creates worksheets for the group and individual writing activities and for the TM activities. The worksheets contain advice on strategy use as identified in E above.

The teacher creates the TM activities on the classroom computer, using a dedicated gap fill package and a package which provides both sequencing and text reconstruction. He or she creates the source text for the gap fill activity and one of the text reconstruction activities in a word processor. He or she also uses the word processor to tidy up the e-mail text used for the sequencing and the other text reconstruction activities. He or she transfers all the texts into the TM package when he or she is happy that they were error-free. When he or she is satisfied that everything is in order, having run each student activity, he or she copies the files from the local hard disc on the classroom computer to the folder set up for the class in question on the network file server.

❼ *Implement the activities*

The students work through the task, and, thanks to careful forward planning, there are few problems. The students feel themselves under some pressure towards the end of the third week, but all manage to complete their assessment task by the appointed date.

❽ *Carry out the assessment*

This is done and, with the exception of students who are absent, everyone manages to hand it in on time.

INFO TECH
Text manipulation

44

⑨ *Evaluate*

The teacher is anxious to know if the task has enabled the students to achieve the objectives listed in Stage 2. He or she takes into account the evidence provided by the assessment task scripts as well as that provided by the responses to the reading and listening tasks. The teacher also takes into account his or her observations made during the two computer room lessons and during the interview sessions in the classroom. He or she finally gets informal feedback from the students, some of whom very much enjoyed the work and felt that they had coped well with the demands of the task. Others found the task a little complicated. A third group felt that there was too much repetition, while a fourth group still doubted their ability to talk and write about jobs despite the exposure to the topic that they had received.

⑩ *Revise*

The teacher felt that the activity had been successful enough to run again the following year. However, he or she plans to look again at the worksheets without delay with a view to editing them in order to respond to some of the students' comments and to sharpen up the focus on the formation of both forms of the future tense as this proved to be the weak spot in the written work, especially with regard to verbs with irregular stems.

45

6 Useful lists and information

TM SOFTWARE PUBLISHERS

The packages referred to in this book are all available for PC compatible computers. Readers are advised to contact the publishers for up-to-date information about availability for Apple Mac and Archimedes computers.

Wida Software Ltd,

2 Nicholas Gardens,
London W5 5HY, UK
Phone: +44 (0)181 567 6941
Fax: +44 (0)181 840 6534
E-mail: widasoft@lang.wida.co.uk
URL: http://www.netkonect.co.uk/wida

Wida publishes the following software referred to in this book:
Authoring Suite
Choicemaster
Gapmaster
Matchmaster
Testmaster

INFOTECH
Text manipulation

Camsoft

10 Wheatfield Close,
Maidenhead,
Berks SL6 3PS
Tel and fax: +44 (0)1628 825 206
E-mail: 100611.671@compuserve.com
URL: http://lupin.csv.warwick.ac.uk/WWW/temps/linguanet/camsoft/

Camsoft publishes the following software referred to in this book:
Fun with Texts
French, German and Spanish text files to go with *Fun with Texts*
Gapkit

Question Mark

Tel: +44 (0) 171 263 7575
E-mail: info@qmark.co.uk
URL: http://www.qmark.com

47

REFERENCES

Atkinson T, *Hands off! It's my go — IT in the languages classroom* (CILT/ NCET, 1992)

Buckland D, *Ideas pack for* Fun with Texts (Camsoft in association with Thomas Nelson, 1992)

Hardisty D and S Windeatt, *CALL* (Oxford University Press, 1989)

Hewer S, *It doesn't interrupt me when I'm thinking — and you do!: an evaluative study of text reconstruction software in foreign language learning.* Unpublished MPhil thesis (University of Nottingham, 1993)

Naiman N, M Frohlich, H H Stern and A Todesco, *The good language learner* (Toronto: Ontario Institute for Studies in Education, 1978; Multilingual Matters, 1996)

O'Malley J M and A U Chamot, *Learning strategies in second language acquisition* (Cambridge University Press, 1990)

Useful lists and information

Rubin J, 'What the good language learner can teach us' in *TESOL Quarterly,* Vol 9, no 1 (1975)

Stern H H, 'What can we learn from the good language learner? in *Canadian Modern Languages Review:* 304–318

Townshend K, *E-mail: using electronic communications in foreign language teaching* (CILT, 1997)

USEFUL URLs (WWW PAGE ADDRESSES)

A Universal Resource Locator (URL) is the address of WWW pages which you type into the top box in your browser tool, followed by Enter to get to the web page itself.

You don't need hundreds of URLs, simply a few with very good links that you can use to 'jump' from to other sites. The following are good 'jump' sites:

48

The Lingu@NET site maintained by CILT and NCET at
http://www.ncet.org.uk/linguanet/index.html

The CTI Centre for Modern Languages, University of Hull at
http://www.hull.ac.uk/cti

A useful site for primary and secondary French is at
http://www.imaginet.french/momes

INFO TeCH
Text manipulation